- Body length: from the tip of the nose to the start of the tail
- Tail length
- Full length: from the tip of the nose to the tip of the tail
- Body height: from the bottom of the feet to the shoulders
- Full height: from the bottom of the feet to top of the head
- Habitat: where the animal lives

Leopard

Body length: 3 to 6 ¼ feet
Tail length: 2 to 3 ⅔ feet
Weight: 100 to 175 pounds
Habitat: Africa, Asia

Gray Wolf

Body length: 2 ⅔ to 5 ¼ feet
Tail length: 1 to 1 ¾ feet
Weight: 80 to 175 pounds
Habitat: Europe, Asia,
North America

Polar Bear

Body length: 6 to 8 ¼ feet
Tail length: 3 to 5 inches
Weight: 900 to 1,700 pounds
Habitat: Arctic Circle

Raccoon

Body length: 1 ⅓ to 2 feet
Tail length: ⅔ to 1 ¼ feet
Weight: 13 to 15 pounds
Habitat: North America,
Central America

Striped Hyena

Body length: 3 ¼ to 5 feet
Tail length: 9 to 14 inches
Weight: 55 to 120 pounds
Habitat: Africa, Asia

More Life-Size Zoo guide

The white box indicates the part of the animal's body that is pictured in the photograph.

Information about the animal in the photograph.
  Approximate age of animal when photographed. (when known)

Scientific name. (the academic name of the animal)

"Time for a Close-Up" More information about what you can see in the picture.

Facts to keep in mind when you see the animal at a zoo.

All of the pictures in this book show the actual size of the animals.

MORE Life-Size ZOO

Lion, hippopotamus, polar bear and more— An all new actual-size animal encyclopedia

Editorial Supervisor of Japanese Edition ● Teruyuki Komiya (Director, Tokyo Ueno Zoo)
Photographer ● Toshimitsu Matsuhashi
Japanese Translation by ● Junko Miyakoshi
English Language Adaptation by ● Kristin Earhart

leopard

A leopard has a different face and spot patterns than a cheetah. They use their keen hearing and eyesight to hunt in the dark night of the jungle.

Time for a Close-Up

Can you see that this leopard has

Black skin around her eyes? And brown eyelashes?

A pink nose?

A wide jaw?

Flower-shaped spots on the middle of her body?

Wide front feet with retractable claws?

Lots of long whiskers on the chin, cheeks, and above the eyes? They can move to help guide the cat at night. Compare them to those on the cheetah, who is active during the day.

Name Sally
Sex Female
Approximate age 5 years
Scientific name Panthera pardus

Leopard facts

1. They are very good at climbing trees. Cubs learn to climb trees very early.

2. They are strong! They can drag their prey fifty feet up into a tree to eat. Their long tails help them balance while climbing.

3. They sometimes jump from the trees to attack.

4. When they don't have trees, any tall place will do. They really like high places.

19

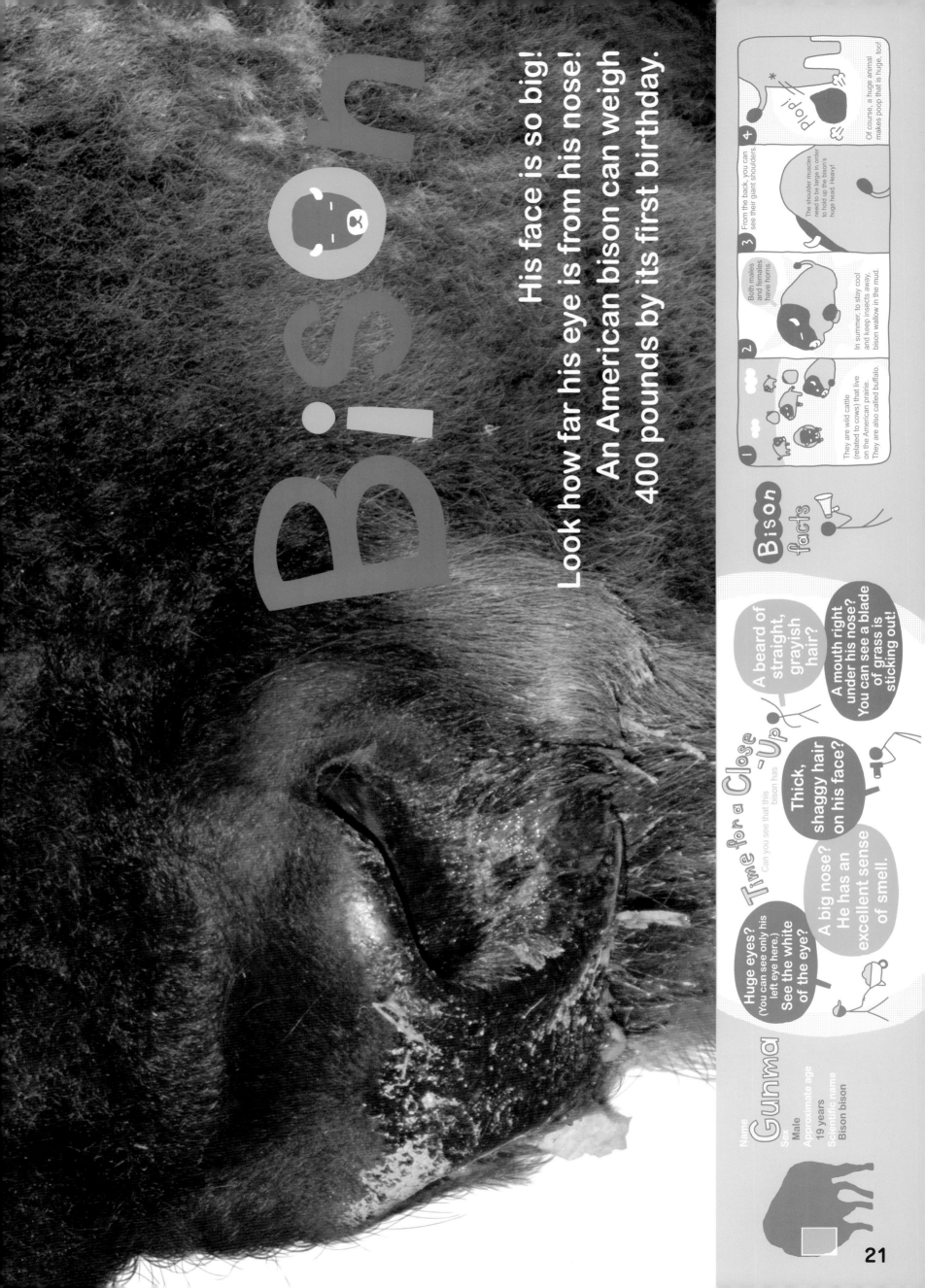

Bison

His face is so big!
Look how far his eye is from his nose!
An American bison can weigh 400 pounds by its first birthday.

Time for a Close-Up

Can you see that this bison has

Huge eyes?
(You can see only his left eye here.)
See the white of the eye?

A big nose?
He has an excellent sense of smell.

Thick, shaggy hair on his face?

A beard of straight, grayish hair?

A mouth right under his nose?
You can see a blade of grass is sticking out!

Name **Gunma**
Sex Male
Approximate age 19 years
Scientific name Bison bison

Bison facts

1. They are wild cattle (related to cows) that live on the American prairie. They are also called buffalo.

2. Both males and females have horns. In summer, to stay cool and keep insects away, bison wallow in the mud.

3. From the back, you can see their giant shoulders. The shoulder muscles need to be large in order to hold up the bison's huge head. Heavy!

4. Of course, a huge animal makes poop that is huge, too! plop!

Seal

This spotted seal has straight,
white whiskers just above his eyes.
They aren't eyebrows,
but special seal antennae that
help him see in the water.

Name

Peace

Sex
Female
Approximate age
10 years
Scientific name
Ursus maritimus

Time for a Close -Up

Can you see that this polar bear has

Deep-brown eyes?

A broad nose? She can smell a seal up to 20 miles away.

Fur that looks white? It is actually clear.

A long beard under her jaw?

Small, rounded ears?

Black skin around her nose? All of her skin is black.

Polar Bear facts

1
They live in the Arctic —on top of the world!

2
They have fur on the bottom of their paws. It keeps them from slipping on ice. There is no fur on their noses, claws, and pads.
nose
claw
pad

3
Polar bears are among the longest bears—growing up to ten feet!

4
They are wonderful swimmers!

Raccoon

Flexible toes let raccoons use their paws almost as well as humans use their hands!

Name
Zeff
Sex
Male
Approximate age
7 years
Scientific name
Procyon lotor

Time for a Close-Up

Can you see that this raccoon has

Pointed ears? The hair around the outside is white, and on the inside it's gray.

A grayish body? The hair is a mix of different colors.

Long, thin toes with long, thin claws?

Black patches around his eyes?

Raccoon facts

They eat with their hands.

Help yourself

Thank you

Raccoon dogs can't hold their food with their hands. They just use their mouths.

I have a striped tail!

27

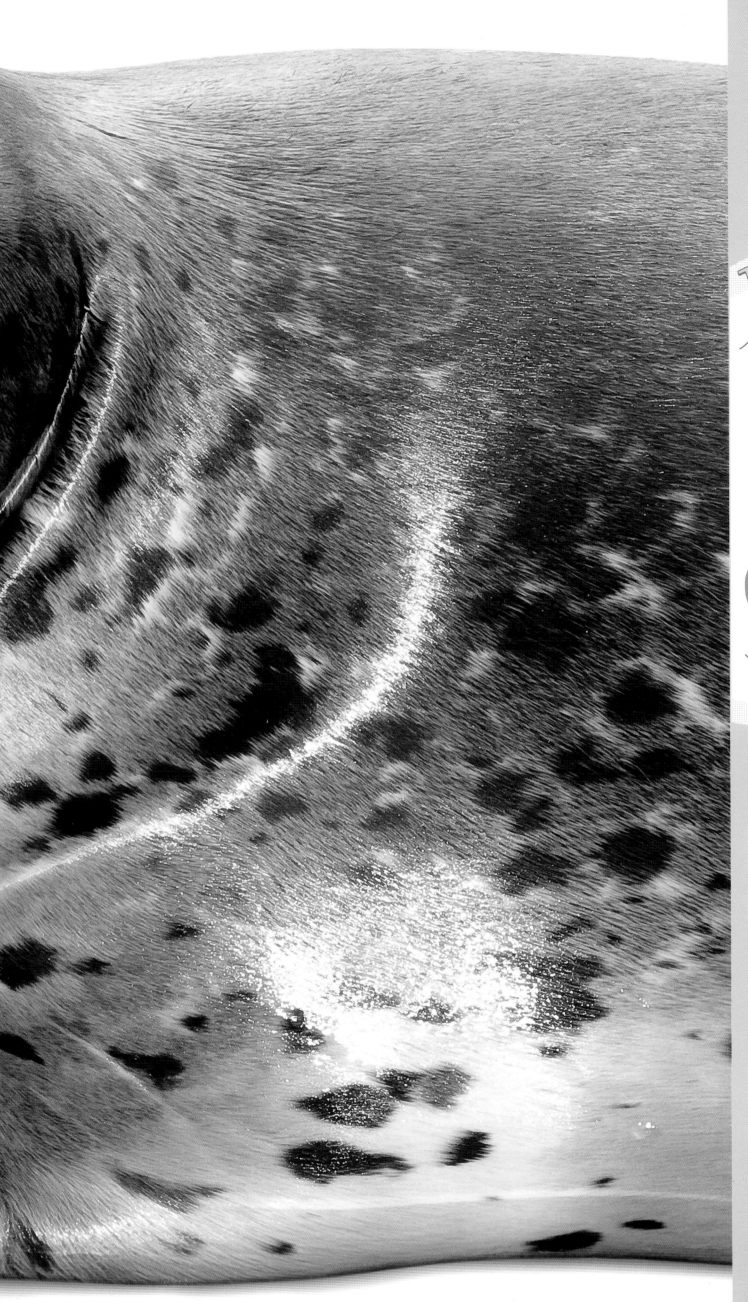

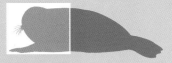

Name
Shouta
Sex
Male
Approximate age
4 years
Scientific name
Phoca largha

Time for a Close-Up

Can you see that this seal has

Lots of whiskers around his mouth?

Nostrils that are open wide? He shuts them when he swims to keep out water.

A hole on the right side of his head? That's his ear!

Five claws on his flipper?

Dense fur all over his body?

Seal facts

1 These amazing whiskers can feel the motion of the seal's prey, so he can track down dinner even in the water.

2 Seals can swim with their eyes closed and use only their whiskers to guide them.

3 They are not as graceful on land as in water, but

4 ...they can really stretch out their necks for a fishy feast.

33

Crocodile

The open jaws of
a crocodile reveal
short teeth, long teeth,
sharp, sharp, sharp teeth!
Snap! Once they chomp down,
they never let go!

Name
Rie
Sex
Female
Approximate age
Unknown
Scientific name
Crocodylus porosus

Time for a Close-Up

Can you see that this crocodile has

No hair at all?
Crocodiles are reptiles. They have scales, unlike mammals, who have hair.

A black mark to the right of the eye? It's her ear hole.

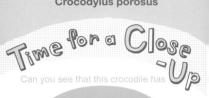

A pupil that isn't round? It opens wide in the dark.

A black mark above the third tooth from the front? This is her nostril.

A pink tongue? Her tongue can close off the back of her throat to keep water from getting in.

Crocodile facts

1. They are reptiles, like snakes, lizards, and turtles.

Reptiles

2. In the wild, they live by the water. They spend most of their time in the water.

3. But they are not like fish. They breathe with lungs. So...

4. ...they have to come up for air. You can often see only their eyes and nostrils sticking out of the water.

35

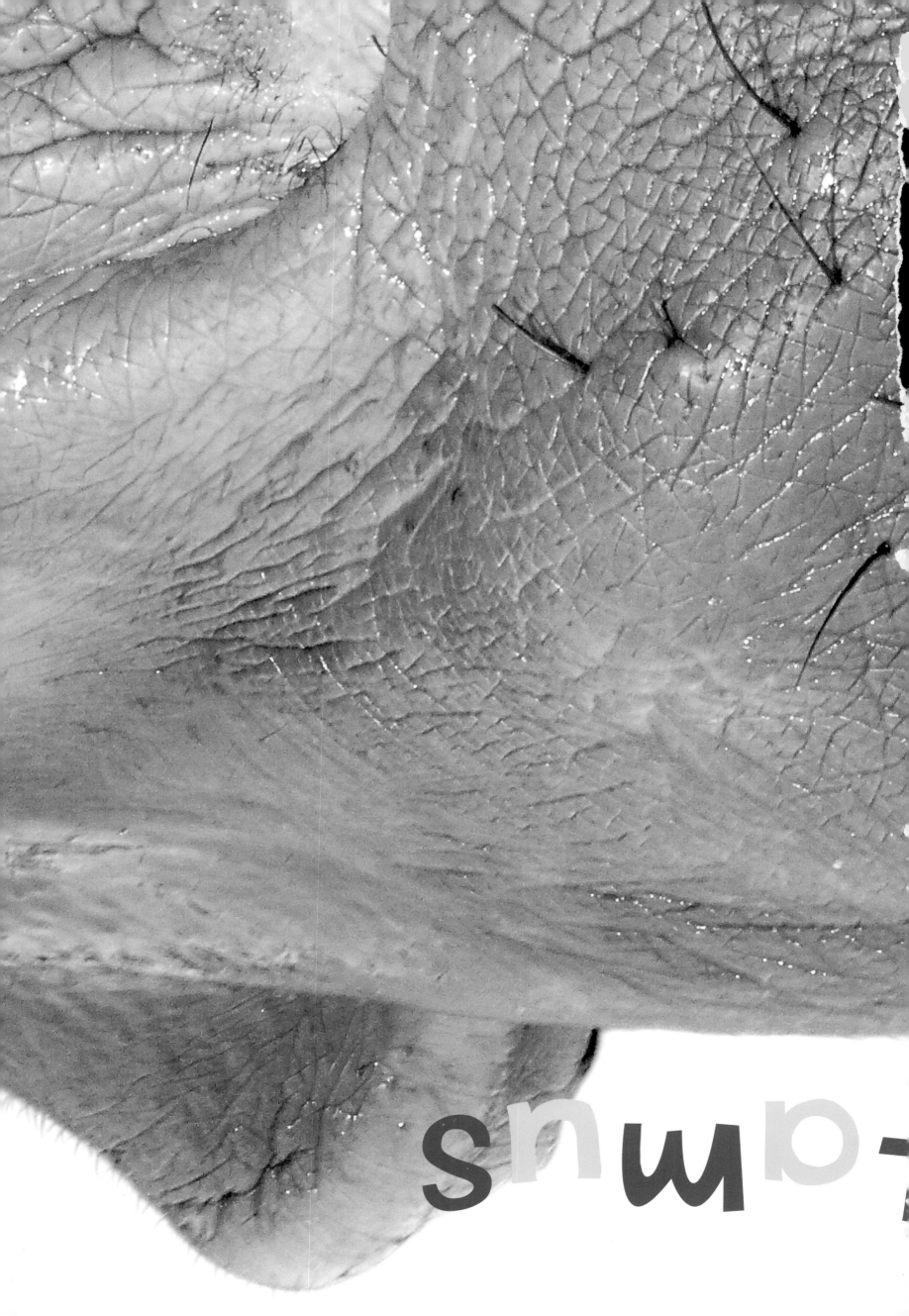

Male orangutans have cheek pads that get larger with age. They are a sign of power.

Name
Didi
Sex
Male
Approximate age
13 years
Scientific name
Pongo pygmaeus

Time for a Close-Up

Can you see that this orangutan has

Eyes like a human's? You can see the pupils and the whites of his eyes.

A flat nose?

A long beard?

Short hair all over his face?

Body hair that looks like the hair on a human's head?

White teeth?

Orangutan facts

1 Orangutans are shy and thoughtful —and hairy.

2 They can pick up food between their fingers and thumbs, just like humans.

3 They can pick their noses, and sometimes eat what they find there!

4 They seem right at home on a tightrope! In the jungle, they live up in the trees, swinging easily from limb to limb.

41

They have wings,
but no feathers.
They fly, but they're not birds.
They eat and sleep upside down.
That's just batty!

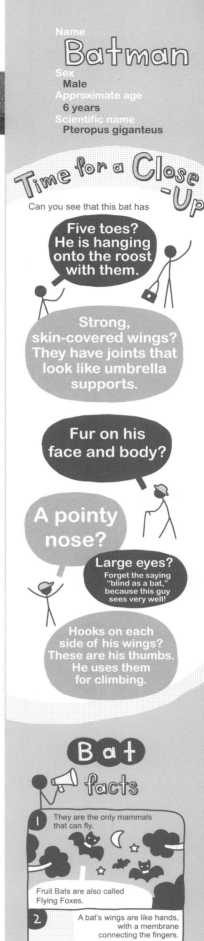

Name
Batman
Sex
Male
Approximate age
6 years
Scientific name
Pteropus giganteus

Time for a Close-Up

Can you see that this bat has

Five toes? He is hanging onto the roost with them.

Strong, skin-covered wings? They have joints that look like umbrella supports.

Fur on his face and body?

A pointy nose?

Large eyes? Forget the saying "blind as a bat," because this guy sees very well!

Hooks on each side of his wings? These are his thumbs. He uses them for climbing.

Bat facts

1. They are the only mammals that can fly.

Fruit Bats are also called Flying Foxes.

2. A bat's wings are like hands, with a membrane connecting the fingers.

Thumb
Index finger
Middle finger
Ring finger
Little finger

3.

They hang upside down except when they pee and poop.

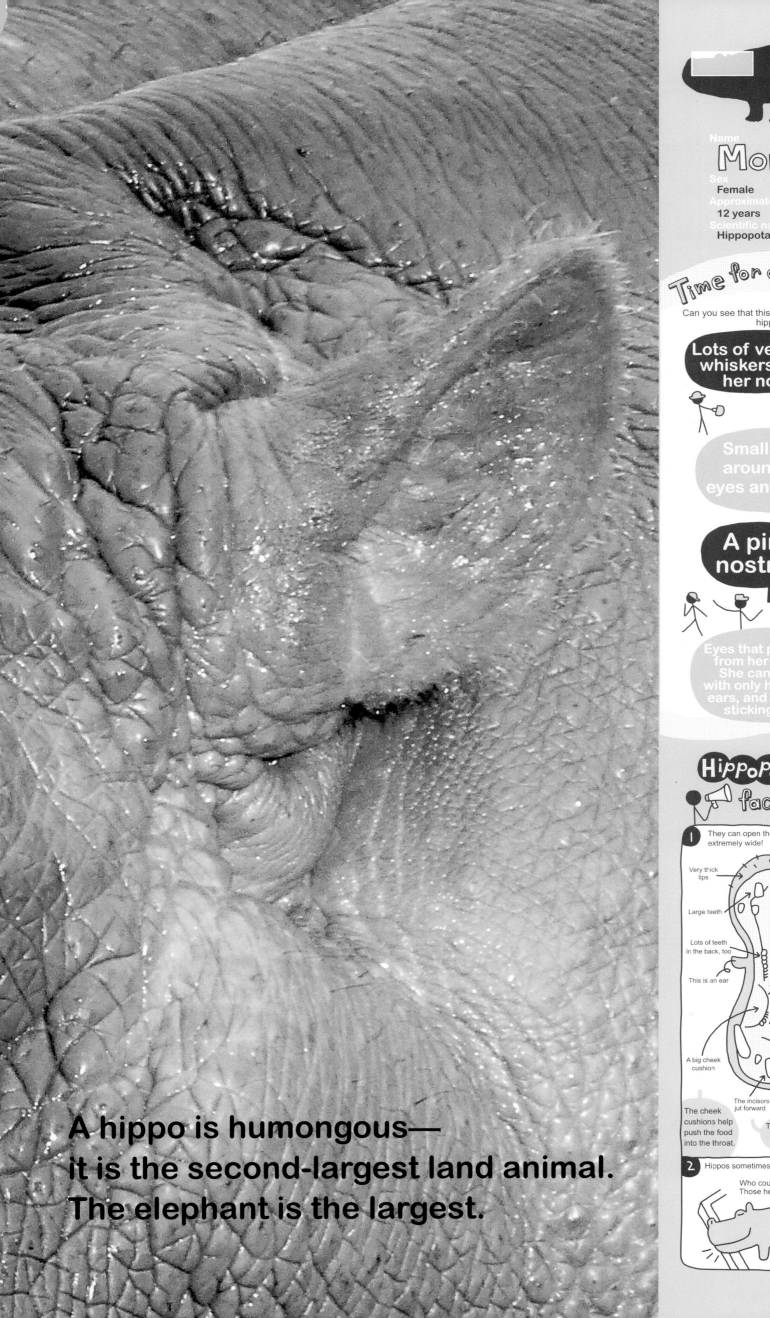

A hippo is humongous—
it is the second-largest land animal.
The elephant is the largest.

Name
Momoko
Sex
Female
Approximate age
12 years
Scientific name
Hippopotamus amphibius

Time for a Close-Up

Can you see that this hippopotamus has

Lots of very thick whiskers under her nose?

Small hairs around her eyes and ears?

A pink nostril?

Eyes that protrude from her head? She can swim with only her eyes, ears, and nostrils sticking out.

Hippopotamus facts

1 They can open their mouths extremely wide!

Very thick lips

Large teeth

Lots of teeth in the back, too

This is an ear

A big cheek cushion

The cheek cushions help push the food into the throat.

The incisors jut forward

A long canine tooth

They are handy for scooping up food.

2 Hippos sometimes rest their heads on the zoo wall. Who could blame them? Those heads look heavy!

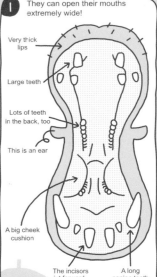

47

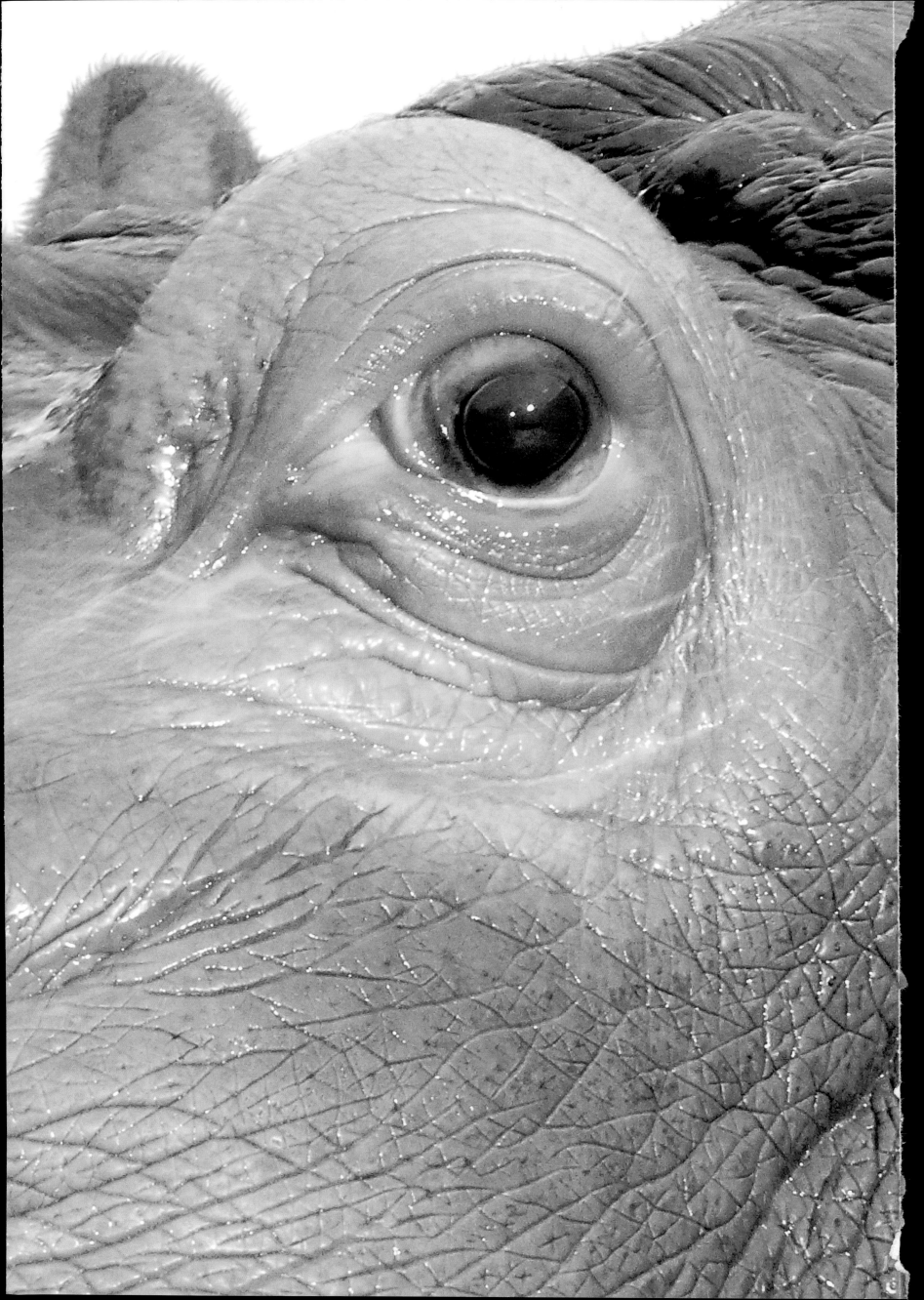

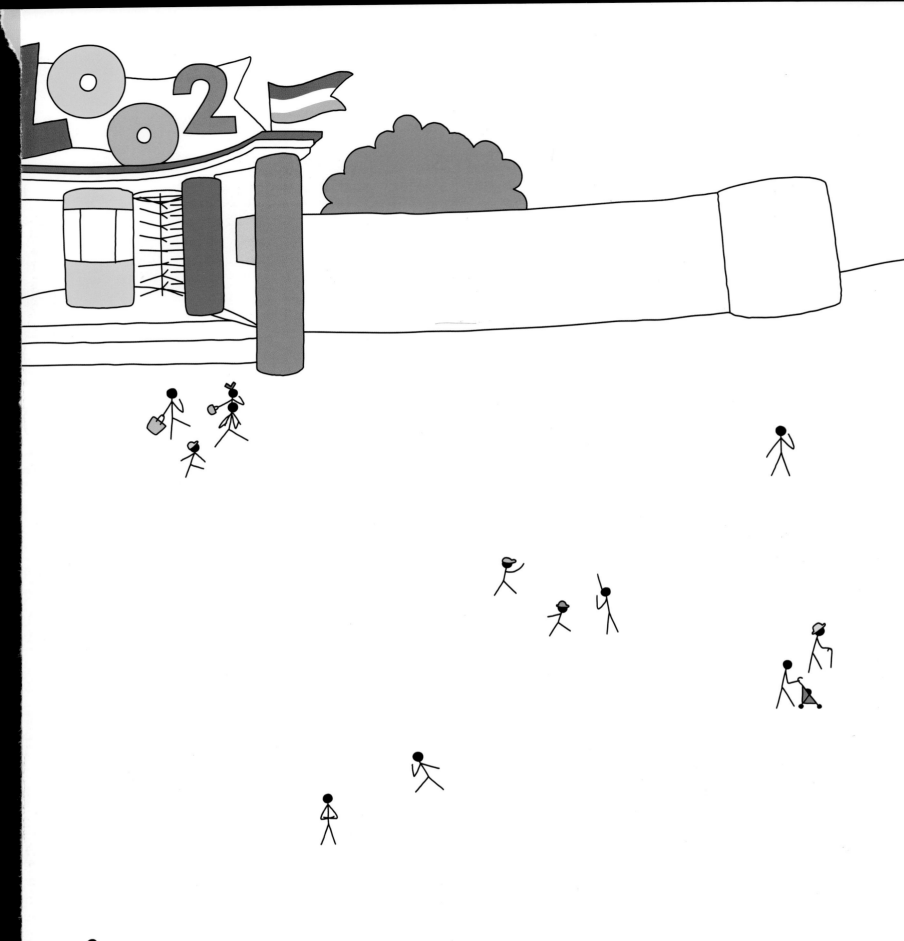

Editorial Supervisor
of Japanese Edition●Teruyuki Komiya (Director, Tokyo Ueno Zoo)

Teruyuki Komiya was born in Tokyo and graduated from Japan's
Meiji University. Currently the director of the Ueno Zoological Gardens,
he has won awards for his research in breeding and care of
animals native to Japan, including the Lesser White-Fronted Goose
(anser erythropus) and the Japanese Hare (lepus brachyurus).

Photographer●Toshimitsu Matsuhashi

Toshimitsu Matsuhashi was born in Japan's Kanagawa prefecture.
He is a freelance animal photographer.

Illustrator ● Akio Kashiwara

Akio Kashiwara was born in Japan's Hyogo prefecture.
He illustrates and designs stationery, books and Web content
as a staff member at Kyoda Creation Co., Ltd.

Japanese edition text ● Masae Takaoka

Masae Takaoka was born in Japan's Ehime prefecture.
She is a freelance editor and writer.

More Life-Size Zoo

Motto! Honto no Ookisa Doubutsu En (More Life-Size Zoo)
© Copyright 2010 / Toshimitsu Matsuhashi
/ Akio Kashiwara (Kyoda Creation Co., Ltd.) / Gakken Co., Ltd.
First published in Japan 2009 by Gakken Co., Ltd, Tokyo
Japanese edition designed by Daisuke Shimizu (Kyoda Creation Co., Ltd.)
Japanese edition text by Masae Takaoka
English translation rights arranged with Gakken Co., Ltd.
through Nextoy LLC

Published by Seven Footer Kids, an imprint of Seven Footer Press,
a division of Seven Footer Entertainment LLC, NY
Manufactured in Shanghai, P.R. China in 01/10
by Stone Sapphire (HK) Limited.
10 9 8 7 6 5 4 3 2
© Copyright Seven Footer Kids, 2010 for English Edition
All Rights Reserved
English adaptation designed by Junko Miyakoshi

ISBN 978-1-934734-19-3

www.lifesizebooks.com

Aquarium this way

Okapi

Body length: 6 ½ to 6 ¾ feet
Body height: 5 to 6 feet
Weight: 460 to 660 pounds
Habitat: Africa (Congo)

Hippopotamus

Body length: 9 ¼ to 13 ¾ feet
Body height: 4 ½ to 5 ⅓ feet
Weight: 3,000 to 7,000 pounds
Habitat: Africa

Bornean Orangutan

Body length: 2 ½ to 3 ¼ feet
Weight: 80 to 170 pounds
Habitat: Southeast Asia

Indian Flying Fox Bat

Body length: ⅔ feet
Weight: 2 to 4 pounds
Habitat: South Asia

Common Wombat

Body length: 2 ⅓ to 3 ¾ feet
Weight: 49 to 86 pounds
Habitat: Australia, Tasmania

Galapagos Giant Tortoise

Shell length: Up to 4 ¼ feet
Weight: 330 to 440 pounds
Habitat: Galapagos Islands (Ecuador)